Story writing

This book belongs to

....

Colour the star when you complete a page.
See how far you've come!

Author: Jon Goulding

How to use this book

- Find a quiet, comfortable place to work, away from distractions.
- This book has been written in a logical order, so start at the first page and work your way through.
- Help with reading the instructions and texts where necessary and ensure that your child understands what to do.
- This book is an introduction to story writing. By working through the activities, your child will learn the skills they need to create their own story.
- Help and encourage your child to check their own answers as they complete each activity.
- Let your child return to their favourite pages once they have been completed. Talk about the activities they enjoyed and what they have learnt.
- Reward your child with plenty of praise and encouragement.
- Learning tips can be found at the bottom of every right-hand page. These give you tips and guidance on how you can help your child with the activities and with writing stories in general.

ACKNOWLEDGEMENTS

Published by Collins
An imprint of HarperCollins*Publishers* Ltd
The News Building
1 London Bridge Street
London
SE1 9GF

HarperCollins*Publishers*
Macken House
39/40 Mayor Street Upper
Dublin 1
D01 C9W8
Ireland

© HarperCollins*Publishers* Ltd 2022
First published 2022

10 9 8 7 6 5 4 3

ISBN 978-0-00-849178-9

The author asserts the moral right to be identified as the author of this work.

All rights reserved. No part of this publication may be reproduced, stored in a retrieval system, or transmitted, in any form or by any means, electronic, mechanical, photocopying, recording or otherwise, without the prior permission of Collins.

Without limiting the exclusive rights of any author, contributor or the publisher of this publication, any unauthorised use of this publication to train generative artificial intelligence (AI) technologies is expressly prohibited. HarperCollins also exercise their rights under Article 4(3) of the Digital Single Market Directive 2019/790 and expressly reserve this publication from the text and data mining exception.

British Library Cataloguing in Publication Data.

A Catalogue record for this publication is available from the British Library.

All images © Shutterstock.com and
© HarperCollins*Publishers*

Author: Jon Goulding
Publisher: Fiona McGlade
Project manager and editorial: Katie Galloway
Design and layout: Sarah Duxbury and Q2A Media Ltd
Cover design: Amparo Barrera and Sarah Duxbury
Production: Karen Nulty
Printed in the United Kingdom by Martins the Printers

Contents

Ideas for writing	4
Characters	6
Settings	8
Paragraphs	10
Improving sentences 1	12
Improving sentences 2	14
Planning a story	16
The opening of a story	18
The story build-up	20
What's the problem?	22
Solving the problem	24
The ending of a story	26
Editing your writing	28
Proofreading	30
Answers	31

Ideas for writing

One of the trickiest parts of writing a story is thinking of a story idea. A simple way of coming up with an idea is to base your story on a story or a situation that you already know.

Characters, settings, events and other details can be changed, and you never know – your new story could be even better than the one you based it on!

1 Draw a line to match each event from the story of 'Jack and the Beanstalk' to the events from a new story idea based on it.

Jack and the Beanstalk	New story
Jack enters the giant's castle.	The dragon wakes up and sees Ella.
Jack climbs a huge beanstalk to the giant's castle.	Ella puts some of the jewels in her bag.
The giant sniffs out Jack and chases him.	Ella scrambles up a dangerous cliff to the dragon's cave.
Jack takes the giant's treasure.	Ella sneaks into the dragon's cave.

2 Think of a story you know and think of three things you could change about it. Complete the table below with your ideas.

For example, Little Red Riding Hood collecting flowers in the forest could be changed to Harry the pirate collecting shells on the beach.

Original story idea	New story idea

3 Think about the new ideas you wrote in Question 2 and consider what else you might change to create your new story. Complete the boxes below with words and pictures.

Drawing pictures can help you remember your ideas and think of new ones.

Where does the story take place?	Who is in the story?

What happens?	How does it end?

It is important to encourage your child to discuss their ideas and say sentences aloud before writing. Sharing ideas can help them to consider what else they can add or if anything needs changing.

Characters

Stories need **characters**, and characters need to be interesting. Characters don't have to be people; they could be animals, aliens, monsters or anything you want them to be.

You need to describe characters so that the reader knows what they **look** like, how they **behave** and how they **feel**. For example:

Ella had short dark hair and a cheeky grin. She was not very tall for an eight-year-old but she was strong and clever. As she looked up at the steep, rocky cliff, she felt excited and a little nervous.

Sometimes, the words a character says give more information about that character as well as helping to tell the story. The words below show that Ella is a determined and brave character.

"I will do this, no matter what," she told herself aloud. "That dragon does not scare me."

Remember to use correct punctuation when using speech in your writing.

1 Read each character description below. Write a sentence using speech to give more information about what each character is like or how they feel.

He was huge. His footsteps were like thunder and he towered over everything.

Titch was small, kind and gentle but right now he felt very worried. His tiny body trembled.

She was upset that there was no more honey. Salty tears rolled down her furry cheeks.

2 In the space below, draw two characters. They could be from a story you know, from the story idea you wrote on page 5, or any two other characters.

Then write a sentence to describe each character: what they look like; how they behave; or how they feel.

| Character 1 | Character 2 |

3 Consider the characters you have described above. Think of something that each of these characters might say that tells the reader something about them.

Character 1

Character 2

Character descriptions can tell the reader much more about a character than simply what the character looks like. Discuss characters with your child, encouraging them to think about feelings, actions, what they might say and how they might say it if they were that character.

Settings

The **setting** is where the story takes place. There might be more than one setting, for example a school and a park or a space rocket and another planet.

You need to describe the setting(s) so that the reader gets a picture in their mind of where the story takes place. **Adjectives** and **adverbs** should be used to create effective descriptions. Adjectives describe **nouns**; adverbs describe **verbs**.

Think about **where** the setting is, for example:

An **enormous** wall of rock stretched **high** into the sky making the mountain almost **impossible** to climb. Just where this **vast** cliff disappeared **eerily** into the clouds, there was a **dark** cave.

adjectives

And think about **what it is like**, for example:

It had a **damp, musty** smell. The floor was covered in the **old** bones and skulls of adventurers who had dared to enter before. The **only** sound was the **gentle** but **unmistakable** breathing of a **sleeping** dragon.

adverbs

1 Think of four adjectives to describe what each setting below looks like.

_____

_____

_____

_____

_____

_____

_____

_____

8

2 Consider one of the settings in Question 1.
Write two sentences:
- one sentence to describe what the setting looks like
- one sentence to describe what it sounds or smells like.

_____

_____

_____

3 Think of a setting from any story you know or from a new story idea you have.
Write adjectives and any other ideas for this setting in the boxes below.

What does it look like?	**What sounds are there?**

What does it smell like?	**How does it feel there?**

Using these adjectives and ideas, write a description of the setting.

_____

_____

_____

_____

_____

Discuss familiar settings with your child, for example, a place they enjoy going. Encourage them to think about what it is like there and discuss it together. Ask them to talk about what can be seen there, the smells, the sounds and how it feels (for example, is it hot, wet, dark, slippery, bright?).

Paragraphs

Paragraphs are important for organising ideas in a story. They break up the writing into blocks of sentences related to the same idea, which makes it easier to read and understand.

In the story of 'Goldilocks and the Three Bears', Goldilocks does three main things: eats the porridge, sits on the chairs and lies on the beds. The sentences for each of these ideas are grouped into separate paragraphs.

Goldilocks saw three bowls of porridge. She tasted each one and decided that Baby Bear's porridge was perfect. Without a second thought, she gobbled it down.

After eating, the mischievous girl needed to sit down. She tried each of the bear's chairs. The smallest was the most comfortable, but she broke it.

    Goldilocks was getting tired, so she tried each of the beds. She decided that the small bed belonging to Baby Bear was perfect and fell into a deep sleep.

> It is common to leave a space between paragraphs to show the reader where each one begins and ends.

> Sometimes, the first word of the paragraph is indented to show the start of a new paragraph.

1 Read the sentences below describing a dragon.

Some sentences belong in paragraph **1**, which describes **what the dragon looks like**. Some belong in paragraph **2**, which describes **what the dragon does**.

Write **1** or **2** after each sentence to show which paragraph it belongs to.

Slowly, the beast lumbered across the vast, dark cave. _____

Its long tongue tasted the air and licked the damp floor. _____

The creature had huge, round eyes on either side of its bony head. _____

A pink, forked tongue poked between sharp, deadly fangs. _____

2 The text below should be split into three paragraphs:
- one about the girl, Ella
- one about the cave
- one about the dragon.

Underline the word that should start each of the three paragraphs.

The small girl crept on silently. Her footsteps were soft and her movements were careful as she entered the dark cave. Inside, the floor was covered with crushed bones. The air was thick with the musty smell of damp and whatever lived in this eerie place. Lying in the darkness in the depths of the cave, the scaly dragon opened one enormous eye. It had sensed movement and was ready to seek out a new victim.

3 Read the text below.

Rewrite the text so that it is in two separate paragraphs. Add one additional sentence to each paragraph.

The beast moved slightly, then stopped and listened. It had heard something in the shadows near to the entrance of its home. Ella hid behind a large rock. She dared not even breathe although her heart was beating fast.

Look at examples of paragraphs in story books with your child. Discuss the main idea of each paragraph and how these ideas change between paragraphs. Support your child by reminding them that when the focus of their writing changes (e.g. a change of setting) they usually need to begin a new paragraph.

Improving sentences 1

Sentences must be **formed and punctuated** correctly. Say your sentences aloud before writing them to check that they make sense.

You can make your sentences more interesting and add more information to them by using:

- **conjunctions** (joining words like 'and', 'but', 'or', 'because')
- **adverbs of time** (words that describe when the action of the verb is carried out, such as 'finally', 'soon')
- **prepositions** (positional words like 'above', 'next to', 'underneath').

For example:

The dragon appeared. It heard something.

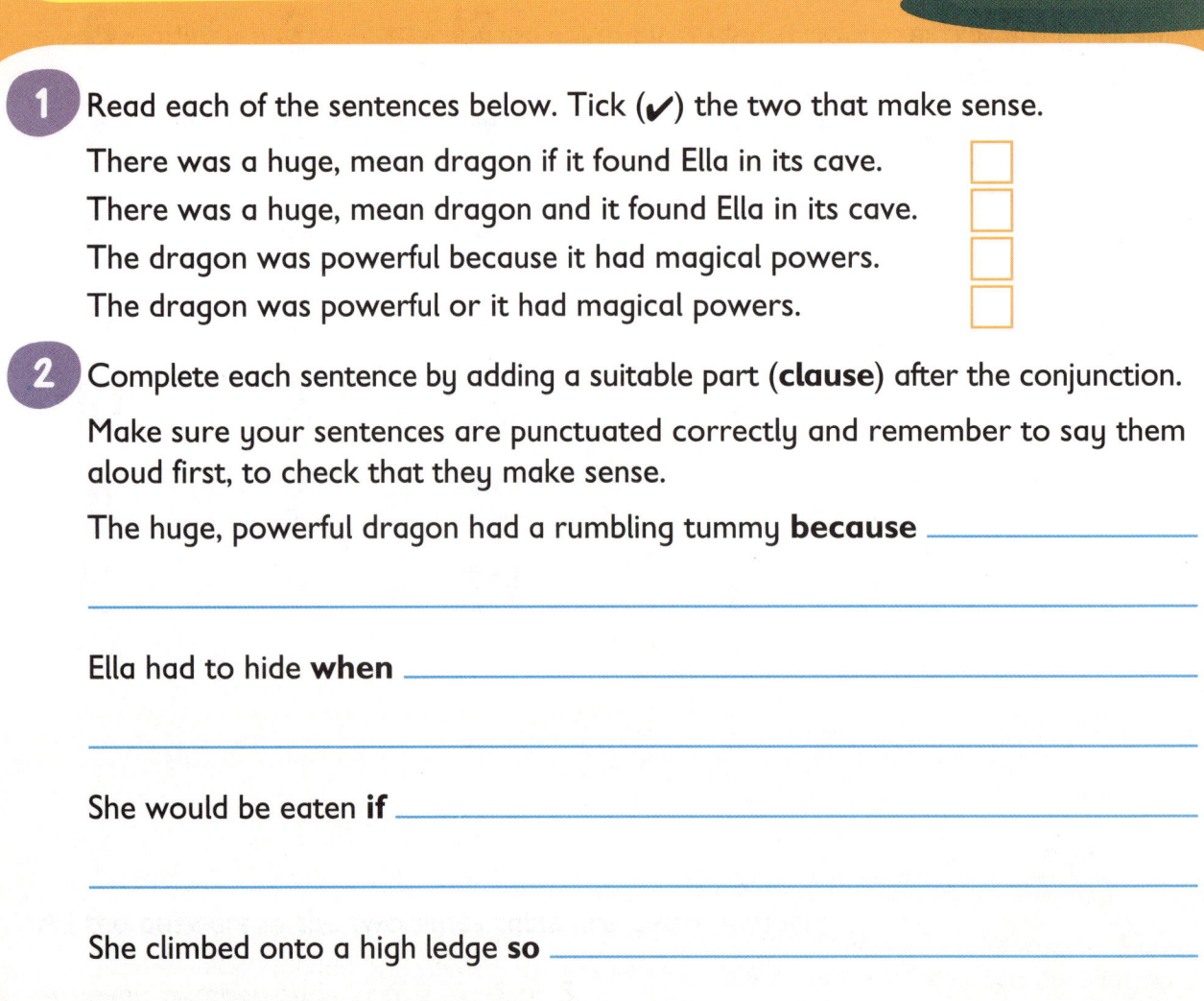

The dragon **immediately** appeared from **behind** a rock **when** it heard something in its cave.

1 Read each of the sentences below. Tick (✔) the two that make sense.

There was a huge, mean dragon if it found Ella in its cave. ☐
There was a huge, mean dragon and it found Ella in its cave. ☐
The dragon was powerful because it had magical powers. ☐
The dragon was powerful or it had magical powers. ☐

2 Complete each sentence by adding a suitable part (**clause**) after the conjunction.

Make sure your sentences are punctuated correctly and remember to say them aloud first, to check that they make sense.

The huge, powerful dragon had a rumbling tummy **because** _____
_____

Ella had to hide **when** _____
_____

She would be eaten **if** _____
_____

She climbed onto a high ledge **so** _____
_____

3 Choose a suitable adverb of time to add to each sentence to give the reader information about 'when'.

        often   **before**   **later**   **soon**

She knew the dragon would see her _____.

If only she had been more careful _____.

_____, she hoped to be able to tell the tale to her friends.

4 Use each of the prepositions below to add more detail about place to the given sentence. Rewrite the whole sentence. The first one has been done for you.

in   **Ella had a strange feeling of fear.**

Ella had a strange feeling of fear in her stomach.

around   **As Ella looked up she could see white clouds.**

_____

_____

on   **Ella was shaking as she sat there.**

_____

_____

beneath   **She knew the dragon was very close.**

_____

_____

> Encouraging the use of adverbs and prepositions to indicate time and place, and conjunctions to extend sentences and ideas, will allow your child to explore ideas and sentences in more detail. Your child should continue to say sentences aloud but should now also consider where, when and why events take place.

Improving sentences 2

To make your story more interesting for the reader, try to use different ways of starting sentences. You could use different sentence lengths too. To avoid repetition, replace nouns with **pronouns** (such as 'she', 'he', 'it', 'they').

Read this passage:

The creature had heard Ella. Ella was scared. Ella climbed onto a high ledge. The creature could see Ella. The creature looked up. The creature gave a loud roar. The creature angrily crawled across the creature's cave.

This passage can be improved by using **adverbials** (adverbs and adverb phrases) at the beginning of some sentences (**fronted adverbials**), using **pronouns** in place of nouns to avoid repetition, and adding more interesting **vocabulary**. For example:

The **hungry beast** had heard Ella. She was **terrified**. **Quickly,** she climbed onto a high ledge. As it looked up, the dragon could now see her and it let out a **bloodcurdling** roar. **Angrily,** the **ravenous** creature crawled across its lair.

Pronoun   Improved vocabulary   Fronted adverbial

1. Rewrite each sentence below with the underlined adverb or adverbial phrase used as a fronted adverbial. This means putting the phrase at the beginning of the sentence and following it with a comma.

The dragon breathed smoke and fire <u>from its angry mouth</u>.

_____

_____

Ella started to tremble <u>fearing for her life</u>.

_____

_____

She <u>suddenly</u> had an idea.

_____

_____

2 Rewrite the paragraph below. Include the same information but use pronouns to avoid repetition and add two fronted adverbials of your own.

> Ella picked up a huge rock. Ella dropped the rock onto the creature below. The creature fell backwards as the rock hit. The dazed creature stared at Ella. Ella had to act fast before the creature recovered.

_____
_____
_____
_____

3 Improve the sentences in the paragraph below about what happens next.

Use at least two fronted adverbials and replace the underlined words with more interesting vocabulary.

> The dangerous creature suddenly <u>jumped</u> at Ella. It knocked her from the ledge. Ella <u>ran</u> towards the cave entrance quickly. She <u>took</u> some of the dragon's treasure. The creature chased her <u>angrily</u>. Ella left the cave and started to climb down the cliff.

_____
_____
_____
_____
_____

> When developing and improving sentences, saying them aloud really helps to recognise the effect of the words that have been used. Encourage your child to try different ways of giving the same information – the ideas can remain but using different words and sentences will help them get a feel for what sounds best. Discuss each sentence with your child.

Planning a story

A simple story structure has a beginning, middle and end, but using a **five-part story structure** can help the ideas in the story to flow.

Part 1: **Opening** – introduces characters and describes the setting
Part 2: **Build-up** – what characters are doing, feeling and what they plan to do
Part 3: **Problem** – an issue that the character(s) faces or that could spoil their plan
Part 4: **Resolution** – how the character(s) overcomes the problem
Part 5: **Ending** – a good or bad outcome, detailing whether the plan was completed

All of these parts need putting together to make a complete story.

1 Think of a story you know. Answer the questions below to help you see how the story fits into a story plan.

For each question, an example answer from the story of 'The Hare and the Tortoise' is given. Write the answer from your story on the line below.

Opening – Who is the character or who are the characters and where is the story set?

Example: Tortoise and Hare   Woodland/meadows

_____

Build-up – What is the character(s) doing and feeling and what is the plan?

Example: Hare is making fun of Tortoise for being so slow. Tortoise challenges Hare to a race.

_____

Problem – What problem does the character(s) face?

Example: Tortoise can't keep up with Hare.

_____

Resolution – How is the problem overcome?

Example: Hare is so far ahead that he decides to take a nap. Tortoise gets past Hare whilst Hare is sleeping.

_____

Ending – How does everything turn out? How do the characters feel?

Example: Tortoise wins the race and is happy to prove Hare wrong. Hare is embarrassed and realises he was wrong for mocking Tortoise.

_____

2 Using the five story parts, plan a story of your own. Remember, it's fine to base your idea on an existing story and just change the details. You could use the idea you had on page 5 or think of a new one.

For each part, write down key words and ideas. Use the questions to help you.

Opening	Who is the character/characters? Where is the story set?	
Build-up	What is the character doing and feeling? What is the plan?	
Problem	What problem does the character face?	
Resolution	How is the problem overcome?	
Ending	How does everything turn out? How does the character feel?	

At this stage, it is fine for children to take ideas from stories they already know and make changes to them, for example, the characters and settings. As they develop their own ideas, encourage them to keep these relatively simple and discuss how well the ideas fit together in the plan.

The opening of a story

Story openings not only have the important job of introducing characters and settings, but they must also grab the reader's attention, making them want to read more.

This story opening introduces the main character and the setting:

Ella was a small girl. She was eight. She stood by a big cliff. High up was a dragon's cave. It contained lots of treasure.

The next example gives the same information but with more interesting detail. It describes the setting in one paragraph and the character in another:

On the edge of a dark forest stood vast walls of rock. High in these cliffs was a cave, its entrance like an eye watching over the land. It was said that inside were gold, jewels and unimaginable wealth. But nobody knew for sure because the cave was also the home of a fierce, evil dragon, and, although many had entered, none had returned.

Ella stared up at the rockface nervously. Although she was a rather small eight-year-old, she was also strong and determined.

1 Look back at your plan on page 17. You can also draw on your ideas from pages 7 and 9.

Think of at least four adjectives to describe your main character and four adjectives to describe your setting.

Character	**Setting**

2 Draw your character and setting here.

3 Write the opening of your story.

Remember to include:

- a paragraph containing a description of your main character(s), including what they look like, their personality and how they feel
- a paragraph describing the setting.

Ask your child to consider what they want the reader to think and feel when they read their writing. Discuss this with your child, encouraging them to think of words and sentences to get this across to the reader.

The story build-up

The story build-up is a place to give the reader some action and tell them about what the character is planning to do.

Remember that there does not need to be any real trouble for the character in the build-up. That will come in the next section, when they are faced with a problem.

Ella knew that this was a dangerous mission. Finding the treasure was one thing but first she had to get to the cave. As she climbed, jagged rocks ripped at her clothes and cut her hands and legs. Looking down, she felt dizzy as the trees of the forest became a dark, green carpet.

She was getting tired but the thought of the treasure kept her going and took her mind off the dragon.

← telling the reader about the mission

← action and feelings

← what it was like for the character

← a reminder of the danger

1 Think about your own story idea and try to answer these questions.

What will your character be doing in the build-up?
_____

Why are they doing it?
_____

How are they doing it? (Think of adjectives and adverbs to describe their actions.)
_____

What is their 'mission' (what they plan to do)?
_____

Why?
_____

2 Think about your story idea and your answers to Question 1. What is your character feeling in this part of the story?

_____

3 Write your own story build-up, using your ideas from the previous questions.

_____

_____

_____

_____

_____

_____

_____

_____

_____

_____

Checklist Have you told the reader what your character is doing? ☐
Have you given an idea of what they plan to do next? ☐
Have you used interesting adjectives and adverbs? ☐
Have you organised your ideas into paragraphs? ☐

Using checklists for story writing is a good way of remembering what to include in a story or parts of a story. However, care must be taken that ideas are not written just to make sure that they can be ticked-off. Discuss with your child whether every piece of information is needed, or whether different information and ideas can be added to their writing.

What's the problem?

In the middle of a story, a problem is introduced. This will usually involve something that might spoil the character's plans.

There may also need to be some description of a new setting as the story moves forward.

Entering the darkness of the cave, Ella could smell decay and damp. The floor was scattered with bones and skulls. She knew that these were the victims of the dragon. She could also see the treasure trove of coins and jewels – they were nearby but far enough away to make it a daunting task to reach them.

Each step she took was slow, careful and silent, but as she moved further from the light, it became harder. As she tried to avoid a large rock across her path, there was a loud crack. Ella had stood on a bone. She froze. As she held her breath, she heard the unmistakable sound of a dragon. She was in great danger and the treasure was now further than ever from her grasp.

This part of the story:

- introduces a new setting (the cave)
- introduces the problem (Ella stands on a bone which wakes the dragon)
- uses paragraphs (one describing the new setting, the cave, and the other introducing the problem).

1 It can be useful to make the reader aware of the danger before there is an actual problem.

In the first paragraph above, copy the two sentences that warn of the danger.

_____

_____

What did Ella do to try to avoid the danger?

_____

What did Ella do to cause the problem in the story problem above?

_____

2 Think about your own story idea.

Write notes for your answers to the questions in the table below, thinking about your own story.

What could be the problem?	What happens to cause the problem?	What does your character do to try to avoid the problem?

3 Write your own problem section for your story.

_____

_____

_____

_____

_____

_____

_____

_____

_____

Discuss the problems in familiar stories. Encourage your child to think about what the problem is and what actually causes it. Next, consider whether the character is doing anything to avoid the problem. Sharing familiar ideas can be a great help in developing your child's own use of language.

Solving the problem

The part of the story where characters have to solve the problem is your chance to include **action** and **suspense**. **Adverbs** are a great tool to use here as they describe verbs (the action) and give more clues to the reader about what is happening.

You need to be clear about the sequence of events in solving the problem. For example:

1. Ella was scared that the dragon had heard her.
2. She climbed on a high ledge to get away.
3. The dragon roared and moved towards her.
4. She dropped a rock on the dragon.
5. She got off the ledge and ran.
6. Ella grabbed some treasure as she went.

These ideas then need to be written in exciting and interesting sentences, for example:

The dragon's sleep was disturbed by the noise. Ella knew the beast had heard her and she started to shake with fear.

1 Write parts 2 and 3 from the events at the top of the page in more detail. Start the first sentence with an adverb, then add verbs in the other spaces.

_____, she _____ up to a high ledge.

The fierce dragon _____ her and let out a deafening roar.

2 Write parts 4 and 5, the resolution, in more detail. Use at least two sentences for each part.

3 Write a list of events for your own story for the part where the problem is solved.

Make sure that at least one event solves, or partly solves, the problem.

Aim for between 4 and 6 events.

1. _____   4. _____

2. _____   5. _____

3. _____   6. _____

4 Using your ideas from Question 3, write the resolution part of your story.

_____
_____
_____
_____
_____
_____
_____
_____
_____
_____
_____
_____

> Discuss familiar stories and encourage your child to read and/or listen to how the author describes events and solves problems for the character(s). Consider your child's own ideas and writing, encouraging them to think about how the events link together.

The ending of a story

Story endings can be tricky to write effectively. It is easy to say that the problem was solved and everyone lived happily ever after, but it is more interesting to include further information.

Leaping between rocks and over bones, Ella stuffed gold coins into her pockets and backpack. At the cave entrance, she swung herself onto the cliff, sliding down her rope at incredible speed. She ran until she could no longer hear the great beast.

This part of the ending links neatly with the resolution — the end of the resolution and the beginning of the ending can be the same part. It gives the last action as the character gets away to safety.

Looking at her treasure, she smiled, but she was not as happy as she'd expected. It had been a fantastic adventure and she was now very rich, but as she made her way home through the dense trees, she knew that she wanted more, and she knew she would be back soon.

The paragraph above tells us how the character feels and lets the reader know that she wants more. This adds interest to the ending as it may not be quite what the reader expected.

1 Complete the table below about a story you know.

What does the main character do at the end of the story?	What words from the story tell you this?
How does the main character feel?	**What words from the story tell you this?**

2 Look back at your plan on page 17 and think about your own story idea.

How does the main character feel at the end of your story?

_____

_____

What does the main character do at the end of your story?

_____

_____

3 Write the ending for your own story, using your answers to Question 2 above to help you.

_____

_____

_____

_____

_____

_____

_____

_____

_____

_____

> As with the whole of the story writing process, discussing the final parts will support and encourage your child to think of an interesting ending. Talking about the endings of stories they know can help them with their ideas. Further discussion about how characters feel, what they have learned, and what they might do next can help endings to develop.

Editing your writing

Editing is a vital part of the story writing process. It involves reading through your writing from the point of view of the reader.

As you read, ask yourself questions such as:

- Does this make sense?
- Does it tell the reader what I want them to know?
- Could I use better, more precise or more interesting vocabulary?
- Could my sentences sound more interesting?
- Have I used paragraphs?

Once you have edited your work, making any necessary changes, read it again to check your improvements.

1. Edit each sentence below by improving the underlined verbs, adverbs and adjectives.

   Ella <u>went quickly</u> through the <u>dark</u> cave, terrified of the <u>big</u> dragon.

   _____

   She climbed <u>quickly</u> down the <u>dangerous</u> cliff, breathing heavily.

   _____

   She ran into the <u>dark</u> forest, <u>happy</u> to be safe.

   _____

2. Choose one of your edited sentences from Question 1 above.

   Now edit it further by changing the order of the sentence and adding further detail if you think it is needed.

   _____

   _____

   _____

3 Read through each part of your own story (pages 19, 21, 23, 25 and 27).

Copy one original sentence from each part of your story in the space below, then write an edited version beneath it.

Opening – Original sentence: _____

_____

Edited sentence: _____

_____

Build-up – Original sentence: _____

_____

Edited sentence: _____

_____

Problem – Original sentence: _____

_____

Edited sentence: _____

_____

Resolution – Original sentence: _____

_____

Edited sentence: _____

_____

Ending – Original sentence: _____

_____

Edited sentence: _____

_____

Encourage your child to edit by reading through each part of their story carefully. Discuss how they feel they could improve sentences by using more interesting words. Ask them how they could make their story sound more exciting to the reader.

Proofreading

An important part of any writing process is **proofreading**. This means checking the writing for any spelling and punctuation errors. Mistakes can easily be made when you are so busy thinking about the story and getting it written down.

Read through your writing very carefully, at least once, making any changes that are needed. If you are unsure about how to spell any words, use a dictionary. To help you check your punctuation, read your writing aloud.

1 Proofread the paragraph below. Rewrite the whole paragraph, changing any spelling and punctuation mistakes.

As goldilocks ran threw the woods, she realised wat a meen girl she had been? She had upset the three bares and know felt very sory. At that moment, yung Goldilocks Decided two become a better person She went home and wrote a letter to the Family Then she made sum porridge. Later that morning she gave the note and the porridge to the Bears before setting off to do some mor good deeds.

2 Proofread the story parts you have written in this book carefully for spelling and punctuation mistakes. Correct any mistakes in your story.

Encourage your child to read carefully when proofreading and to use a dictionary where necessary. Give praise for the effort they have put into their writing and ideas. Perhaps your child might like to write out their story again so that all the parts run on. They may also wish to add pictures and think of a title.

Answers

Pages 4–5

1. Jack enters the giant's castle. — Ella sneaks into the dragon's cave.
   Jack climbs a huge beanstalk to the giant's castle. — Ella scrambles up a dangerous cliff to the dragon's cave.
   The giant sniffs out Jack and chases him. — The dragon wakes up and sees Ella.
   Jack takes the giant's treasure. — Ella puts some of the jewels in her bag.
2. Child's own ideas written.
3. Child's own pictures drawn and notes written.

Pages 6–7

1. Examples:
   "I'm coming to eat you all!" he bellowed.
   "I'm terrified," he whispered.
   "I'm so hungry," she sniffed.
2. Two characters drawn. One sentence written to describe each character: what they look like; how they behave; or how they feel.
3. Speech written for each character.

Pages 8–9

1. Examples:
   First setting: green, pretty, peaceful, pleasant
   Second setting: welcoming, busy, lively, colourful
2. Examples:
   The café had big windows and lots of outdoor tables, filled with chatty customers. Laughter and chatter, combined with upbeat music and the hiss of the coffee maker, made the café lively and noisy.
3. Adjectives and other ideas written for child's own choice of story setting. Description using full sentences of child's own choice of story setting.

Pages 10–11

1. Slowly, the beast lumbered across the vast, dark cave. 2
   Its long tongue tasted the air and licked the damp floor. 2
   The creature had huge, round eyes on either side of its bony head. 1
   A pink, forked tongue poked between sharp, deadly fangs. 1
2. <u>The</u> small girl crept on silently. Her footsteps were soft and her movements were careful as she entered the dark cave. <u>Inside</u>, the floor was covered with crushed bones. The air was thick with the musty smell of damp and whatever lived in this eerie place. <u>Lying</u> in the darkness in the depths of the cave, the scaly dragon opened one enormous eye. It had sensed movement and was ready to seek out a new victim.
3. Examples:
   The beast moved slightly, then stopped and listened. It had heard something in the shadows near to the entrance of its home. It started to shift towards the sound. Ella hid behind a large rock. She dared not even breathe although her heart was beating fast. She could hear the dragon stirring.

Pages 12–13

1. There was a huge, mean dragon and it found Ella in its cave. ✔
   The dragon was powerful because it had magical powers. ✔
2. Examples:
   The huge, powerful dragon had a rumbling tummy **because** it hadn't eaten for two weeks.
   Ella had to hide **when** the dragon woke up.
   She would be eaten **if** the dragon managed to find her.
   She climbed onto a high ledge **so** the dragon wouldn't be able to see her.
3. soon; before; Later
4. Examples:
   As Ella looked up she could see white clouds all around the top of the mountain.
   Ella was shaking as she sat there, high on the ledge.
   She knew the dragon was very close somewhere in the cave beneath her.

Pages 14–15

1. From its angry mouth, the dragon breathed smoke and fire.
   Fearing for her life, Ella started to tremble.
   Suddenly, she had an idea.
2. Example:
   Hurriedly, Ella picked up a huge rock. She dropped it onto the creature below. It fell backwards as the rock hit. Furiously, the dazed creature stared at Ella. She had to act fast before he recovered.
3. Example:
   Suddenly, the dangerous creature lurched at Ella. It knocked her from the ledge. Quickly, Ella raced towards the cave entrance. She grabbed some of the dragon's treasure. The angry creature chased her furiously. Ella left the cave and started to climb swiftly down the cliff.

Pages 16–17

1. Answers based on child's choice of story.
2. Plan of child's own story idea.

Pages 18–19

1. Four adjectives written to describe child's own character idea and four adjectives written to describe child's own setting idea.
2. Pictures drawn of child's own character and setting ideas.
3. Opening paragraph written about child's own character idea and opening paragraph written about child's own setting idea.

Pages 20–21

1.–3. Child's own answers about their story idea.

Pages 22–23

1. The floor was scattered with bones and skulls. She knew that these were the victims of the dragon.
   Ella tried not to make any noise.
   She stood on a bone, which made a loud cracking noise.
2. Child's own answers about their story idea.
3. Problem section of child's own story idea written.

Pages 24–25

1. Examples:
   Carefully, she climbed up to a high ledge. The fierce dragon spied her and let out a deafening roar.
2. Examples:
   She grabbed a large rock from underneath her. Mustering as much energy as she could, she hurled it hard at the dragon. Without looking back, Ella jumped off the ledge. She ran as fast as her legs would carry her, determined to get away.
3. List of events from child's own story ideas.
4. Resolution section of child's own story idea written.

Pages 26–27

1. Child's answers about their own choice of story.
2. Child's own answers about their story idea.
3. Ending of child's own story idea written.

Pages 28–29

1. Examples:
   Ella dashed hastily through the shadowy cave, terrified of the enormous dragon.
   She climbed nimbly down the treacherous cliff, breathing heavily.
   She ran fast into the gloomy forest, relieved to be safe.
2. Example:
   Breathing heavily, she climbed nimbly down the steep, treacherous cliff, her heart in her mouth.
3. Child's edited sentences from their own story.

Page 30

1. As <u>G</u>oldilocks ran <u>through</u> the woods, she realised <u>what</u> a <u>mean</u> girl she had been<u>.</u> She had upset the three <u>bears</u> and <u>now</u> felt very <u>sorry</u>. At that moment, <u>young</u> Goldilocks <u>decided</u> <u>to</u> become a better person<u>.</u> She went home and wrote a letter to the <u>family</u> <u>then</u> she made <u>some</u> porridge. Later that morning<u>,</u> she gave the note and the porridge to the <u>b</u>ears before setting off to do some <u>more</u> good deeds.
2. Child's own proofreading of their story idea.